THE BATTLE OF KOSOVO

The Battle of Kosovo

TRANSLATED FROM THE SERBIAN BY
JOHN MATTHIAS AND VLADETA VUČKOVIĆ
Preface by Charles Simic
Afterword by Christopher Merrill

Swallow Press

Ohio University Press
Athens

Swallow Press/Ohio University Press, Athens, Ohio 45701
Printed in the United States of America
All rights reserved. Published 1999

Swallow Press/Ohio University Press books are printed on acid-free paper ∞ ™

05 04 03 02 01 00 99   5 4 3 2 1

ACKNOWLEDGMENTS

Some of these translations have appeared previously in *The Kenyon Review, Poetry World,* and *Prospice.* "The Kosovo Maiden" and "To V.V.: On Our Translations of the Kosovo Fragments" appeared in John Matthias's book *Northern Summer: New and Selected Poems,* Anvil Press and Swallow Press, 1984.

Library of Congress Cataloging-in-Publication Data

The Battle of Kosovo.

    Bibliography: p.
1. Epic poetry, Serbian—Translations into English. 2. Folk-songs, Serbo-Croatian—Translations into English. 3. English poetry—Translations from Serbo-Croatian. 4. Kosovo, Battle of, 1389—Poetry.
I. Matthias, John, 1941–   . II. Vuckovic, Vladeta.
PG1465.B38   1987   891.8/211   87-10061
ISBN 0-8040-0897-3 (pbk.)

CONTENTS

Preface

I was ten years old when I first read these heroic ballads. It was during one of the bleak postwar winters in Yugoslavia. There was not much to eat and little money to heat our apartment properly. I went to bed as soon as I got home from school, to keep warm. Then I would listen to the radio and read. Among the books my father left was a thick anthology of "Serbian Folk Poems." That's what they were called. In the next few years I read the whole volume and some of the poems in it at least a dozen times. Even today I can still recite passages from my favorite ballads. None of this, of course, was in any way unusual. Every Serbian loves these poems.

The Kosovo Cycle I learned to appreciate somewhat later. I first fell in love with the ballads that describe the adventures and heroic feats of various rebels during the Turkish occupation. They are "action packed," as they used to say on movie posters. The Turks are the cruel conquerors and the Serbs are either clever slaves or outlaws.

In the ballad *Little Radojica*, for example, the inmates of Aga Bećir Aga's notorious prison are rejoicing because their pal, little Radojica, still hasn't been caught. But then, he is. They throw him in the deepest dungeon among the now despairing prisoners and he figures out what to do. He tells his comrades to inform the Aga as soon as the day breaks that he died during the night. That's what they do. The Turks carry Radojica, who is pretending to be dead, into the prison yard. The aga takes one look and tells his servants to throw the stinking corpse into the sea. But now his wife and daughter show up. The wife says that Radojica is only pretending, that they should build a fire on his chest to see if he stirs. They do, and he doesn't. Then she asks them to hammer nails under his fingernails. Still Radojica doesn't budge. The aga has had enough, but the wife has one more idea. She asks her daughter to dance with her girlfriends around the dead man, and the daughter, we are told, is very pretty. There follows a wonderful description of the daughter's flowing robes and jingling bracelets as she dances. Poor Radojica is opening one eye and his mouth is curling up into a grin. The daughter sees this and throws her veil over his face. Radojica is finally thrown into the sea where he manages to swim out to a far rock to nurse his wounds and wait for the night to come. The aga is having supper with his family when he breaks in, kills the parents, frees the prisoners, and takes the daughter to be his wife.

I hope the bare plot outline of *Little Radojica* conveys how entertaining these poems are. What is missing, of course, is the building suspense, the wonderful descriptive details, as well as the humor and

7

poetry of the piece. Even in these later ballads the complexity of the vision, for which the Kosovo Cycle is famous, is present. It's not that Turks are all bad and the Serbs all heroes. The view of history and the appraisals of the individual figures found in the poems are full of ambivalences and psychological savvy. These rebels are often ordinary brigands out to enrich themselves. They collaborate with the enemy and seem to have every ordinary human weakness. If they're heroes, it's in spite of themselves. Neither the tribe nor the hero are idealized. The world view of these poems is different from that of the Kosovo Cycle where the mythic and epic dimensions reign supreme. Nevertheless, they both touch the earth. A sense of proportion and a sense of realism is what they share.

II

One day in school, in what must have been my fifth or sixth grade, they announced that a *guslar* would perform for us. This was unexpected. Most city people in those days had never heard a *gusle* being played, and as for us kids, brought up as we were on American popular music, the prospect meant next to nothing. In any case, at the appointed time we were herded into the gym where an old peasant, sitting stiffly in a chair and holding a one-stringed instrument, awaited us. When we had quieted down, he started to play the *gusle*.

I still remember my astonishment at what I heard. I suppose I expected the old instrument to sound beautiful, the singing to be inspiring as our history books told us was the case. *Gusle*, however, can hardly be heard in a large room. The sound of that one string is faint, rasping, screechy, tentative. The chanting that goes with it is toneless, monotonous, and unrelieved by vocal flourishes of any kind. The singer simply doesn't show off. There's nothing to do but pay close attention to the words which the *guslar* enunciates with great emphasis and clarity. We heard *The Death of the Mother of the Jugovići* that day and a couple of others. After a while, the poem and the archaic, other-worldly-sounding instrument began to get to me and everybody else. Our anonymous ancestor poet knew what he was doing. This stubborn drone combined with the sublime lyricism of the poem touched the rawest spot in our psyche. The old wounds were reopened.

The early modernist Serbian poet and critic, Stanislav Vinaver, says that the sound of *gusle* is the sound of defeat. That, of course, is what the poems in the Kosovo Cycle are all about. Serbs are possibly unique among peoples in that in their national epic poetry they celebrate defeat. Other people sing of the triumphs of their conquering heroes while the Serbs sing of the tragic sense of life. In the eyes of the universe, the poems tell us, the most cherished tribal ambitions are nothing. Even the idea of statehood is tragic. Poor Turks, the poet is suggesting, look what's in store for them.

Vinaver also speaks of "heroic spite." Achilles rebelled against all the Greek chieftans; Gilgamesh against the gods. The poet of the Kosovo Cycle rebels against the very idea of historical triumph. Defeat, he appears to be saying, is wiser than victory. The great antiheroes of these poems experience a moment of tragic consciousness. They see the alternatives with all their moral implications. They are free to make a fateful choice. They make it with full understanding of its consequences.

For the folk poet of these poems, true nobility and heroism comes from the consciousness of the difficult choice. They say the old Greeks had a hand in this. Very possibly. The world from which these poems came didn't change that much from the days of the Greek dramatists.

There's also the Christian context, but even that doesn't fully explain the poems' view of the human condition. The Serbs do not think of themselves as Christian martyrs, or as chosen people with a mystical destiny. The ballads are remarkable for their feel for actual history. The mythical is present but so is realism. This is the fate of all the small peoples in history and of all the individuals who find themselves the tragic agents and victims of its dialectics.

III

Everyone in the West who has known these poems has proclaimed them to be literature of the highest order which ought to be known better. And, of course, there have been many translations since the mid-nineteenth century. Except for one or two recent exceptions, they do not resemble the originals at all. We either get Victorian Homer or just plain incompetence.

There's no question that the poems are hard to translate. Their literary idiom is somewhat unfamiliar. There's nothing quite like it in English or other western European literatures. One has to invent equivalents rather than to just recreate familiar models.

Perhaps the main stumbling block is prosody. The ten-syllable line in Serbian is a mighty force. Each syllable is audible and distinct. The trochaic beat sets a fairly regular and steady pace. The translator immediately runs into a problem. The lines in English translation tend to be much longer. Both the conciseness and the syllabic quality of the verse are lost. One is left with a lot of words per line and no meter to

9

recreate the narrative drive of the original.

Then there's the problem of the diction. The early translations tend to poeticize and idealize what is really a model of economy and understatement. This is not Ossian, or even Tennyson. In the Kosovo Cycle there's an absolute minimum of verbosity and epic posturing.

What John Matthias and Vladeta Vučković have done strikes me as an ideal solution. Breaking the line at the caesuras gives it a lilt, an anticipation at the break, a "variable foot" effect in the manner of William Carlos Williams's later poetry, that captures the pace of the narrative. Matthias is a superb craftsman. His intuition as to where and how to adjust the tempo of the various parts of the poem to achieve a maximum narrative and dramatic result almost never fails him. He grasps the poetic strategies of the anonymous Serbian poet as much as Pound did those of Chinese poetry.

The other great accomplishment of these translations is in the language. When it comes to fate and tragedy, the original seems to be telling us, use only absolutely necessary words. The clarity, the narrative inevitability, and the eloquence and poetry of the Kosovo Cycle come through in these translations. I don't know any better ones. If the Serbian heroic ballads are indeed great poetry, as people keep saying, you will get a good taste of that greatness here.

Charles Simic

10

Introduction

The Serbian Empire reached its brief moment of glory in the mid-fourteenth century during the reign of Tsar Stefan Dušan. Two centuries earlier, the Nemanja dynasty was born when its founder, Stefan Nemanja, obtained recognition from the Emperor of Byzantium as grand *zhupan* of Serbia in 1159. Nemanja's younger son, Stefan the First-crowned, and his remarkable brother Sava, established the kingdom on a firm military, cultural, and religious basis after the Crusaders' victory over the Byzantines at Constantinople in 1204. Stefan became king in 1217, and by 1219 Sava had succeeded in establishing an autocephalous Serbian Orthodox Church with himself at its head as archbishop. By 1331, following the violent reign of Milutin and the murder by his son of Stefan Dechanski, Stefan Dušan, patricide and political visionary, was king, becoming tsar in 1346. He pacified Bulgaria by marrying the Bulgarian tsar's sister, conquered much of Macedonia, defended himself against the aggressive Hungarians, and aspired to the crown of Byzantium while ruling over a rapidly expanding empire which stretched from the Sava to the Gulf of Corinth, from the Bulgarian border to the Adriatic Sea. Rebecca West has famously compared him with Elizabeth I, saying that upon his sudden death in 1355, and with the resulting factional struggles which occurred during the reign of his son Uroš and coincided with the Ottoman invasions culminating in the battles of Marica and Kosovo, it is probable that as much was deducted from civilization "as the sum of England after the Tudor Age."[1]

The chief contenders in the factional struggle after 1356 were two members of the Serbian nobility, the brothers Vukašin and Uglješa. By 1371 they had recognized too late the necessity of unity against the Turks, and perished together fighting Sultan Murad's marshal, Evrenos, at the Battle of Marica. In this year Uroš also died without an heir. Now the claimants for the throne of Serbia were three: Marko, the son of Vukašin; Tvrtko, the king of Bosnia; and Lazar, the nobleman who would lead the armies at the Battle of Kosovo and become the much-mythologized and Christ-like tsar of the epic songs. The son of Vukašin experienced a similar metamorphosis and became, in time, the epic hero Marko Kraljević.

"The image of disaster of the Battle of Kosovo has lived for centuries in Serbian literary and oral traditions with the elusive vividness of a hallucination," writes Svetozar Koljević.[2] History, in fact, is a good deal less informative than are poetry, folklore, and song; less vividly hallucinatory, it is more like a mirage. What we know is that nine years after the Battle of Marica, Lazar managed to bring his own forces together with those of his son-in-law, Vuk Branković, Tvrtko of Bosnia, and other powerful Serbian and Croat leaders for a decisive battle on Kosovo field, the Field of Blackbirds, on St. Vitus's Day, 1389. The fortress at Niš had fallen to Murad twenty-five days before at the end of his steady progress toward the Danube and Sava across the valley of the Morava. The Kosovo battle resulted in heavy losses on both sides, but seems to have been devastating for the Serbs in that most of their leaders and nobility were killed or driven into exile. Sultan Murad was assassinated behind his lines by a Serbian knight, Miloš Obilić, and Lazar was captured and beheaded by the Turks. The epic songs give two contradictory reasons for the Serbian defeat: the treachery of Vuk Branković – which seems to have no basis in fact – and Lazar's decision before the battle to sacrifice his earthly kingdom for a heavenly kingdom, to lead his men into battle knowing what the tragic outcome was to be as one might lead a host of martyrs consciously into a conflagration. Although full Turkish domination of Serbia was actually only very slowly achieved by Murad's successors, and while the final and conclusive battle was not fought until 1459 for the fortress at Smederevo on the Danube, it is Kosovo which has lived in the popular imagination and in epic poetry as the moment of annihilation and enslavement. Bernard Johnson has compared the "popular belief in 'a great nation strangled at birth'" to "the legends surrounding the Battle of Hastings . . . or Roncesvalles."[3] One might also invoke *The Gododdin* of Aneirin and the Welsh defeat at Catraeth or, it goes without saying, the fall of Troy. Vasko Popa, who like Ivan Lalić and Miodrag Pavlović, brings the myth of Kosovo forward from the epic songs into the Jugoslav poetry of our own day, writes in *Earth Erect*:

> A field like no other
> Heaven above it
> Heaven below[4]

II

Scholars are still uncertain at what point precisely the songs of Kosovo began to be sung. The decasyllabic poems emerging from a patriarchal village context were preceded by, and evidently for a while developed parallel to, the poems in lines of fourteen to sixteen syllables emerging from a feudal context in an urban Adriatic setting known as *bugarštice*. This tradition may have been uprooted from its natural home in the medieval Serbian courts and obliged to go into exile with those who patronized it and became, in some cases, its epic heroes. Or it may have originated with the fugitives in exile. At any rate, after the Turkish victories at Marica, Kosovo, and finally Smederevo, many Serbs, including numbers of the surviving nobility, migrated to Bosnia, Herzegovina, and along the Adriatic coast, some of them settling in or near the Republic of Ragusa, later to become the city of Dubrovnik.

Dragutin Subotić believes that the strong influence of Italian literature and popular poetry in Ragusa – the Sicilian originals of current *strambotti* and *rispetti*, for example, as much as Ariosto and Tasso – together with the appearance there of troubadour poetry (perhaps through the agency of Petrarch) and certain Castilian *romances* with their dominant theme of the struggle between Christianity and Islam, acted on the memories of educated Serbian exiles to produce the first *bugarštice* based on accumulating oral histories and folklore sometime in the late fifteenth century.[5] Many of these poems dealt with the struggles between Serbs or Croats and the Turks, although most of them sang of battles which were fought well after Kosovo. Svetozar Koljević, observing that poetic conventions will naturally enough be slow to develop in a migratory culture, also dates the appearance of the *bugarštice* about Kosovo and later battles with the Turks from the Adriatic coast in the fifteenth century, although he minimizes the Italian influence and doesn't consider that of the troubadours, stressing instead his view that epic singing had always been cultivated in the medieval Serbian courts. He argues that, with the breakdown of feudal civilization and increasingly powerful, systematic, and coordinated Turkish domination in the Balkans, the epic songs of men who had achieved a professional status in the feudal context also, as it were, broke down. This left a debris of themes, techniques, phrases, and epic formulas that were inherited by illiterate village singers who adapted them – not without a certain initial clumsiness showing where and how the metamorphosis had taken place – to the characteristic decasyllabic song accompanied by the *gusle*, the single-stringed instrument which became ubiquitous among peasants, shepherds, and outlaws during the late phase of Turkish rule.[6] Decasyllabic songs of a lyric kind – including the so-called "women's songs" treating domestic and erotic subjects – may have been sung in villages and fields for a thousand years. The line proved ultimately to be more flexible and muscular in its handling of the epic subjects than had been the line of the *bugarštice*. Furthermore, it positively flourished. Although we have only about a hundred feudal *bugarštice* that have been preserved in written texts, there are literally thousands of the decasyllabic songs. And it is the decasyllabic songs that express most eloquently the tragedy of Kosovo.

If the traditions of the feudal *bugarštice* and the decasyllabic village song are undeniably interconnected, and if there is a case to be made for a connection between the *bugarštice* and a written literature, whether Italian, Spanish, or even French, the question of any direct relationship between the decasyllabic village singing and a written literature is still a matter of debate. Albert B. Lord in particular, arguing for the purity of the oral stream, denies any relationship at all between the two traditions in his famous study, *The Singer of Tales*, and declines to find much significance in the written compositions apparently modeled on oral forms by Šiško Menčetić and Džore Držić in the fifteenth-century or in the eighteenth-century literary epic written in a combination of prose and decasyllabic lines by Andrija Kačić-Miošić.[7] Subotić, on the other hand, believes that "both currents flowed into each other: heroic songs chanted by the *guslari* found their way into literature, while written stories reached the *guslari*, who turned them into decasyllabic lines."[8] Koljević, too, believes in what he calls "the rich and fascinating interplay of literary and oral culture in the central Balkans." Taking them more seriously as evidence of reciprocity between the written and the oral traditions than does Albert Lord, Koljević cites the poems of Džore Držić, and he notes that parts of Ivan Gundulić's epic *Osman* found their way from seventeenth-century Dubrovnik into oral poems around Kotor.[9] Lord himself, in fact, acknowledges that decasyllabic passages from Kačić-Miošić's poem later "entered into the oral tradition whence they had not come."[10] For our purposes, however, what needs now to be observed is the function of the decasyllabic oral song itself as a weapon in the hands of an occupied people leading to the moment of its systematic documentation and literary retrieval by Vuk Karadžić during the nineteenth century rebellion against the Turks.

III

If I were asked to produce a single image among those known to me most resonant of the suffering endured by the Christian Slavic population during the long night of Turkish rule in the Balkans, I would not hesitate a moment before choosing a scene in the third chapter of Ivo Andrić's sweeping historical novel, *The Bridge on the Drina*.

Muhammad Sokolović (later Sököllü), the son of a Bosnian peasant who was among the children regularly taken from their parents and borne off to Istanbul at an early age to swell the ranks of the Janissary corps or to do the work of slaves, rose to the remarkable heights of grand vizier in 1565 and governed the Turkish empire until his death in 1579. Wishing to be remembered in his homeland, he ordered the construction of the immense stone bridge across the Drina at Višegrad which resulted in years of forced labor for the inhabitants of the area and particular hardship for the members of the unconverted Christian *rayah*. In Andrić's novel, one of the peasants pressed for labor on the bridge attempts to sabotage the work, spreading a rumor that a *vila*, the often malicious fairy of Balkan folklore, was destroying the bridge. Caught at night prizing cut and mortared stones into the river, he is tortured and sentenced to be impaled at the highest point of the construction work on a larded wooden stake eight feet in length and pointed at the end with iron. The slow, anatomically detailed description of the execution is an agony; one feels the shaft in one's own entrails. A Gypsy executioner hammers the stake from the anus through the man's entire body, without piercing any of the important organs, until it exits at the right shoulder by the ear. The peasant, slowly dying between noon and sunset, is placed erect on the bridge, spitted like a roasting pig on his stake. To children gathered on the riverbank, it looked as if "the strange man who hovered over the water [was] suddenly frozen in the midst of a leap." If impaling under the Turks was about as common as crucifixion under the Romans, there is also little doubt with whom this martyred peasant in his death is meant to be compared.

Against such suffering as the impaled man is emblem of, what recourse? In the same chapter of Andrić's novel, there is another scene. Exhausted men from the Christian *rayah*, worn down by forced labor on the bridge, sit around the dying embers of a fire in a large stable drying their wet clothes and worrying about the work that's left undone, the autumn plowing, in their villages. A recently impressed Montenegrin is among them. Taking a *gusle* from the pocket of his cloak, he applies resin to the string while one of the peasants stands guard outside. "All looked at the Montenegrin as if they saw him for the first time and at the *gusle* which seemed to disappear in his huge hands . . . At last the first notes wailed out, sharp and uneven." Excitement in the stable rises. Everyone is motionless, intent now on the tale which is about to be sung.

> Suddenly, after he had more or less attuned his voice to the *gusle*, the Montenegrin threw back his head proudly and violently so that his Adam's apple stood out in his scrawny neck and his sharp profile was outlined in the firelight, and sang in a strangled and constrained voice: A-a-a-a a-a-a-a- and then all at once in a clear and ringing tone:

15

> The Serbian Tzar Stefan
> Drank wine in fertile Prizren,
> By him sat the old patriarchs,
> Four of them . . .

> The peasants pressed closer and closer around the
> singer but without making the slightest noise; their
> very breathing could be heard. They half closed
> their eyes, carried away with wonder . . . . The
> Montenegrin developed his melody more and more
> rapidly, even more beautiful and bolder, while the
> wet and sleepless workmen, carried away and
> insensible to all else, followed the tale as if it were
> their own more beautiful and more glorious
> destiny.[11]

So it must have been by the sixteenth century in the areas which Koljević calls "the cradle of decasyllabic village singing"[12] – Bosnia, Hertzegovina, and Montenegro – where Serbian migration had carried the epic debris of the *bugarštice*. Many of the songs, he believes, were sung about Kosovo, though none could yet be written down under the eyes of the Turkish authorities. As Andrić portrays the singing in his novel, it is somehow both an escape from pain and a stimulus to action (the sabotage on the bridge follows immediately). As if one were to think at one and the same time listening to the *guslar*: "Lazar is dead, and there is nothing to do but rest in the song of Tsar Stefan who ruled in glory long before the Turks," and "Lazar is dead – but let us avenge him and be free in a kingdom like Tsar Stefan's was before the Turks!", the objective conditions of history at any particular time determining which side of the contradictory response was likely in the end to predominate. One might legitimately compare the analogous power of certain American Negro spirituals simultaneously to provide consolation and assure an enslaved community that a day of reckoning would come for the oppressors. "When Israel was in Egypt's land," they sang, although in the case of the Balkans it was Egypt that was in the land of Israel.[13]

The day of reckoning for the Turks began in 1804 with the first Serbian uprising and coincided with the career of Vuk Stefanović Karadžić, the great linguistic reformer and collector of oral literature. Karadžić was born in 1787 in a village on the east of the Macava Plain which is itself bordered on the west by the Drina. His family, having come from Herzegovina, moved to Tršić in the Serbian hill-country on the edge of Bosnia, insuring that the future scholar would grow up not only in the region which had become the heart of decasyllabic village singing, but also where he would experience both the excitement and the cruelties of heroic life later to be sung or spoken for his dictation by Filip Višnjić, Tešan Podrugović, and others who fought in or followed the fortunes of the revolt. Conscripted as a clerk by Djordje Čurčija, a leader of the uprising in his region, Karadžić served in his undisciplined army until it was defeated in the summer of 1804 by a Turkish assault from Bosnia across the Drina into Loznica and on to Šabac. Karadžić's description of Čurčija's death at the hands of men fighting under Nenadović, another leader of the revolt who had persuaded Karadjordje that Čurčija was guilty of treachery and obtained his superior's permission to have him killed, is as gruesome as anything in the bloodiest of heroic songs.[14]

By 1813 the first insurrection was put down by the Turks, who were only driven out of Serbia for good during the second revolt led by Miloš Obrenović beginning in 1815. Like thousands of other Serbs, Karadžić crossed into Austrian territory where, before settling in Vienna, he recorded epic poems by singers who, like himself, had fought in the rebellion. Returning to the monastery of Šišatovac in Srem province in 1814 and 1815, he systematically set about his life-long task of taking down the songs of medieval Serbia, the Battle of Kosovo, Marko Kraljević, and the recent insurrection itself from men who had inherited the tradition of decasyllabic singing from the peasants, outlaws, border-raiders, merchants' sons, shepherds, and occasional blind visionaries living under Turkish rule. Filip Višnjić, Karadžić's most famous singer, actually personifies this last popularly stereotypical image of the guslar, while Tešan Podrugović, who prefered to speak rather than to sing his poems, was indeed an outlaw driven into the woods for killing a Turk. Podrugović joined the uprising in 1804 and returned to fight again when the second revolt broke out in 1815, literally in the midst of dictating poems. Most of the great songs about Marko Kraljević in Karadžić's collection were recited by Podrugović, and many reflect the characteristics not only of the long tradition he had inherited, but also of his own powerful personality. A unique individual talent also modifies tradition in the case of Old Milija, especially in his wonderful version of *Banović Strahinja*, and perhaps also Old Raško and Stojan the Outlaw.

There were, of course, written records of the oral poems before Karadžić began to publish systematically in 1814. Single *bugarštice* had been written down as early as 1555 and, by 1720, the Erlangen Manuscript had recorded decasyllabic heroic poems. Alberto Fortis's Italian *Travels in Dalmatia*, containing *The Wife of Asan-aga* both in the original and in Italian translation, followed in 1774, reaching Goethe

17

whose German version, *Klaggesang von der edlen Frauen des Asan Aga*, appeared in Herder's *Folksongs* in 1778 and drew the attention of poets and intellectuals all over Europe to the Serbian oral tradition. Karadžić's work as a collector, however, coinciding with a nationalist revolt and with the enthusiasm of the Romantic movement for folk poetry of all kinds, and reinforced by his reformation of the Serbian language itself based on the conviction that Serbian should be written as it was spoken by the people and preserved in the people's poetry, made an unprecedented and lasting impact. Support in the enterprise came at once from the deeply influential Jacob Grimm, and later from a wide range of poets, critics, and translators including Goethe, "Talvj" (Therese Albertina Louisa von Jacob), Wilhelm Gerhard, Sir John Bowring, Adam Mickiewicz, V.G. Belinsky, and Alexander Pushkin (who, along with translating some of Karadžić's actual texts, was deceived by Prosper Mérimée's synthetic confection called *La Guzla*). Karadžić himself, busy with other projects, often lacking money, and crippled by a mysterious withered leg that required the use both of a wooden attachment and a crutch, traveled for years throughout Serbia, Croatia, Montenegro, Bosnia and the Adriatic coast recording for posterity both epic and lyrical oral poems. Not until 1862 was the definitive four-volume Viennese edition of *Serbian Folk Poems* complete. Although there have been other collections since, none has replaced it.

Like virtually all other serious translators of the Kosovo poems, we have used the versions collected by Vuk Karadžić. Interestingly, only one of our selections from Karadžić's second volume containing decasyllabic poems about Kosovo, its anticipation and its aftermath, was taken down from one of his most famous singers – Podrugović's *Tsar Lazar and Tsaritsa Militsa*. Along with the five eloquent fragments dictated to Karadžić by his father and an unknown singer's version of *Musić Stefan*, several of the best known poems – *The Downfall of the Kingdom of Serbia, Tsaritsa Militsa and Vladeta the Voyvoda, The Kosovo Maiden*, the post-Kosovo *Death of Duke Prijezda* and probably also an unknown singer's *The Death of the Mother of the Jugovići* – were written down from the memorized recitations of old blind women, some of them associated with monasteries in Srem. It is difficult to know what to make of this. Before Karadžić's time, these songs, or versions of them, doubtless would have been sung to the *gusle* by male singers such as Filip Višnjić. It is hard to know when and how the old women became custodians of several of the greatest epic poems in the tradition. Koljević calls the part they play "a completely different story . . . which is not usually fully recognized" and finds their greatest contribution to

18

be "their sense of the distant past [which] seems to be stronger and sometimes more accurate than that of other singers."[15] But the old women were not, in fact, singers. Nor was Karadžić's father. Nor even, technically, was Podrugović when he spoke his poems. We have arrived, therefore, at a point where it is necessary to say a few words about the technique of oral poetry and about what happens when an oral poem is dictated, written down as a fixed text, and translated into another language – in our case English.

IV

Most American and British readers who are acquainted with the tradition of decasyllabic epic poetry know it from the work of Milman Parry and Albert B. Lord culminating in Lord's *The Singer of Tales*, the Harvard collection of *Serbocroatian Heroic Songs* taken down by modern recording techniques, and Bela Bartok's musical transcriptions of the actual singing and playing of the *gusle*. Although Karadžić often stressed that the poems of his singers were improvised rather than memorized, it required the work of Parry and Lord to demonstrate in technical terms the manner in which an apprentice singer slowly learned a full vocabulary of epic formulas and phrases in terms of which he would create orally a poem which he had learned orally in the act of oral performance. In his chapter on "Writing and Oral Tradition," Lord likens the act of writing down an oral poem to photographing Proteus; a particular version is artifically preserved while the song itself continues to change its shape in subsequent performances.[16] Podrugović's version of *Tsar Lasar and Tsaritsa Militsa* would have been different in some respects on Wednesday from the version he dictated to Karadžić on Tuesday, although there also would have been many stable elements – runs of lines, and of course the epic formulas themselves – remaining intact from one performance to another. And yet even by Karadžić's time, the fluidity of the oral tradition had begun in some ways to harden; Podrugović himself no longer sang but spoke his poems, and the Kosovo tales dictated by the old blind women sitting in the shade of monasteries had been memorized word for word – like Paternoster, as S. Radojčić has remarked.[17]

This introduction is not the place to take up in detail the Parry-Lord theory of oral composition or the recent chapters in the debate it has generated.[18] It is enough that the reader understand that, in the case of each poem, he is reading a written English version of a written Serbo-Croatian version of an oral poem which, in the hands of another singer, or in earlier times, or in the hands of the same singer (with the exception

19

of the old women) at a later time, would have been differently performed in certain significant respects.

Looking at a printed text in the absence of actual singing to the *gusle*, the translator is confronting a verbal rhythm which is insistently trochaic. Each pentameter line, moreover, is invariably end-stopped, and there is always a caesura pause after the fourth syllable. Between them, Lord and Bartok have shown how subtle and flexible this line becomes through an interplay of melody and text in actual performance. Accents are not stressed with equal intensity, iambs and dactyls may be imposed and extra syllables supplied by words without meaning. The last syllable is often distorted or swallowed, and the penultimate is inclined to become the most prominent; further, the singer does not usually observe the caesura (although its existence is very real to him).[19] Written down in cold print, however, the line to be translated is somewhat distressingly regular:

Pódĭ/zé sĕ// Ćrňo/jécĭc/Ívŏ.

Predictably enough, different translators have dealt with the line in different ways, and solutions range from attempts to write English trochaic pentameter without making the heroic poems sound like *The Song of Hiawatha*, to imitations of William Morris's meter in his translation of *Sigurd the Volsung*, simple syllable-counting, prose that respects the integrity of each line and attempts to achieve occasional rhythmical effects, and prose printed in paragraphs.[20] Our own solution has been to break the original line into halflines, vary the position of the caesura (to coincide with the line breaks, which in fact sometimes make for only a visual pause in reading), and strive for a flexible and melodious iambic rhythm. I don't think there is any getting away from the fact that it is pretty much only the iambic pentameter that is capable of expressing traditional heoric emotions in English. (Even Christopher Logue's Homer is often heavily iambic.) We do use fragments of trochaic meter when possible in a dominantly iambic context, but we do not at any point attempt to reproduce a strict decasyllabic line. Although we cannot provide on the page the rhythmic subtleties that an actual oral performance accompanied by the *gusle* would make manifest, we are able to strive, at any rate, for variety and flexibility within a norm. Again, we do not use a strict syllable count in our line, and we do not always end-stop. The line length varies from four to seven feet; the norm is five. The pause at the line break varies from long, to short, to merely visual.

If this approach proves to be controversial among purists, I suspect

20

that other decisions which we have made along the way will be even more so. I will note just three more possible issues here and relegate the rest to a footnote. (1) We call the Serbian Tsar *both* Lazar *and* Lazarus, depending upon rhythmical considerations. Although rather odd on the face of it, I think this works out perfectly satisfactorily in practice. It amounts to treating the name as if it could be inflected in English (which it can be and is in Serbo-Croat). (2) It is characteristic of these poems for the tense to shift back and forth from past to historic present somewhat in the manner of the *Poema del Cid*.[21] We follow the original changes of tense in our translation only when the effect of doing so is interesting or meaningful in English and never when it is merely conventional or might create confusion. (3) We now and then use Serbian and English titles interchangeably. The "Tsar" is also called "Prince" and "Lord." A "knight" may well walk into a poem and a "voyvoda" or a "duke" walk out of it.[22] But at this point I should stop saying "we" and say "I." My collaborator, who has been gratifyingly forbearing throughout our several years of work together, is not responsible for some of the more radical liberties taken with some of our texts. It would take far too much space to explain and defend all of these, and I hope it will not seem disingenuous to say that it was in fact the tradition of oral composition and improvisation itself that made me feel free to add occasional lines and epic formulas of my own, eliminate others, lengthen and shorten lines, and even leave untranslated the uninteresting conclusions of *The Downfall of the Kingdom of Serbia* and *Marko Kraljević and the Eagle*. (This last, I know, is not properly speaking a Kosovo poem; but I want to include it as a transition to the next major cycle and a promise to myself to keep working.) I have also been perfectly willing to borrow phrases and diction from other translators when neither I nor my collaborator could think of anything better. These small acts of plagiarism, too, seem to me perfectly consistent with a tradition which does not conceive of or reward originality according to the terms in which we have come to understand it. I have tried, in the end, to produce final versions of the poems translated here in a readable, rhythmical English – an English which I have tested myself in oral performance in England, America, and Jugoslavia.

I must give Vladeta Vučković the last word. I have tried to communicate something of the nature of our collaboration in my poem to him appearing as an Afterword to our translations. For Vučković, the Kosovo poems exist, as they do for Andrić, Popa, Lalić, and Pavlović, as part of a tradition which he himself continues in his work. There is an irony and sadness in his poems which is difficult to render in English, but which, I think, provides a usefully provocative contrast to Andrić's vision of the *guslar* quoted earlier from the pages of *The Bridge on the Drina*. His long poem about Serbian mythology and history is written both in verse and prose. This is part of the conclusion to section one:

> What Serbs remained got up from the plain and counted each other and called out, but nobody got any answers. No one came to help them, and so the Turkish Power passed the border of the First Dimension. After a while there remained almost nothing at all: dust and ashes, vain repentance, late remorse, and the heavy blackness of total defeat
> . . . .
>
> The Serbs quieted down, but they did not shut their mouths. Idled by the time on their hands they started to sing and sang themselves hoarse in endless poems accompanied by the mourning sounds of the sobbing gusle. The blind guslars gazed into the future, and those who could see covered themselves out of shame and became the leaders of the blind. But what kind of music is this, my poor soul, reduced to just one string!

John Matthias

Notes

1. Rebecca West, *Black Lamb and Grey Falcon* (1942; reprint, London: Macmillan Publishers, 1982), p. 900.
2. Svetozar Koljević, *The Epic In The Making* (Oxford: Oxford University Press, 1980), p. 154.
3. Bernard Johnson, Introduction to his translation of Miodrag Pavlović's Selected Poems, *The Slavs Beneath Parnassus* (St Paul: New Rivers Press, 1987), p. 20.
4. Vasko Popa, *Collected Poems 1943–1976, trans. Anne Pennington (Manchester, England: Carcanet Press, 1978), p. 109.*
5. *Dragutin Subotić, Yugoslav Popular Ballads: Their Origin and Development* (Cambridge: Cambridge University Press, 1932), pp. 149–60.
6. Koljević, pp. 31–66.
7. Albert B. Lord, *The Singer of Tales* (1960; reprint, New York, Atheneum, 1980), p. 135.
8. Subotić, p. 90.
9. Koljević, pp. 2, 33–34.
10. Lord, p. 136.

11. Ivo Andrić, *The Bridge on the Drina*, trans. Lovett F. Edwards (1959; reprint, Chicago: University of Chicago Press, 1977), p. 34.
12. Koljević, p. 300.
13. Of the major European epics, *The Battle of Kosovo* is probably most like *The Song of Roland*, where the epic hero is also a Christian martyr. But in another sense *Kosovo* is unique. It is both fragmentary and open-ended. The slow accretion of parts and episodes, what the French call *fermentation épique*, was incomplete by the time the individual sections began to be written down. Or, if one wishes to think of the poem being "completed" (to the extent that *Roland* was completed by the time it was written down), it is completed only by the cycles which follow it – by the poems of Marko Kraljević and the poems about the revolt against the Turks – and by the events of 1804–1813 which produced both the last great singers and many of the tales they sang.
14. Duncan Wilson, *The Life and Times of Vuk Stefanović Karadžić* (Oxford, Oxford University Press, 1970), p. 43.
15. Koljević, p. 319.
16. Lord, p. 124.
17. S. Radojčić, cited in Koljević, p. 320.
18. See especially Koljević's concluding chapter, "Technique and Achievement," pp. 322–43.
19. Lord, pp. 38–42.
20. Translations, imitations, versions and travesties of the Kosovo, Marko Kraljević, and other epic poems have been published in English beginning in 1827 with Sir John Bowring's *Servian Popular Poetry*. (Sir Walter Scott's version of Goethe's version of "The Wife of Asan-aga" was published only in 1924.) The interested reader should consult the work of Owen Meredith, J.G. Lockhart, Elodie Lawton Mijatovich, Helen Rootham, G.R. Noyes, Woislav M. Petrovitch, R.W. Seton-Watson, W.A. Morison, D.H. Low, and Nada Ćurčija-Prodanović. Representative selections by many of the above are quoted for comparative purposes in Subotić, and a bibliography of all translations published before 1975 is available in *Yugoslav Literature in English: A Bibliography of Translations and Criticism*, edited by Vasa D. Mihailovich and Mateja Matejić. The most recent translation is *Marko The Prince*, by Anne Pennington and Peter Levi (London: Duckworth, 1984).
21. W.S. Merwin notes in his translation (*Poem of The Cid*: New York, Meridian Books, 1975, p. xxx) that the purpose of using the historic present was "to bring details into the foreground" while the past tense was intended to "hold them at a remove." This sometimes also seems to be the case in the *Kosovo* poems.
22. To continue, but also to exonerate my collaborator: (4) I have felt free to add and subtract formulaic adjectives almost at will. What was "the white castle at Krushevats" may well become "the castle at white Krushevats," etc. (5) I have sometimes stretched the line so far beyond ten syllables that I have had the uneasy feeling I was remaking bugarštice out of decasyllabic poems. (6) Sometimes two lines of the original become one line in English when there is a great deal of repetition of the formulaic matter. (7) I have worked up the last fragment – "Who is that fine hero" – almost as a lyric. This may be going too far. (8) I have gratuitously included tags from Yeats and Pound: "Raging in the dark" and "I have seen what I have seen." This *is* going too far.

A Note on Pronunciation

In her own frustrated note on pronunciation in *Black Lamb and Grey Falcon*, Rebecca West observes that "the Cyrillic alphabet is designed to give a perfect phonetic rendering of the Slav group of languages, and provides characters for several consonants which other groups lack. The Latin alphabet can only represent these consonants by clapping accents on other consonants which bear some resemblance to them; and Croatian usage still further confuses the English eye by using *c* to represent not *s* and *k* but *ts*, and *j* for *y*." She concludes that "in practice the casual English reader is baffled by this unfamiliar use of what looks familiar and is apt to pass over names without grasping them clearly." In the context of poetry one must add "without *hearing* them clearly," and worry more about the English (and American) ear than about the eye. Because line after line of the poems translated here might otherwise be distorted by mishearing names of people and places, we have decided to transliterate where it seems necessary to produce a fluent reading. This has meant that names of heroes such as Miloš Obilić and places such as Niš and Peć have been transliterated as Milosh Obilich, Nish and Pech. But there are places where the system breaks down. Rebecca West gave up trying to transliterate "Sarajevo" and "Skoplje" and was regularly plagued by the problem of liquid consonants which the Latin alphabet must indicate by adding *j* to *l* and *n*. The lesson seems to be that one should leave the *j* alone and remind the reader that *j* is usually pronounced *y* as in yard (the exceptions being after *a*, when it is pronounced *ie* as in tie, and in combination with *l* or *n* where *lj* sounds like *lli* in million and *nj* like *gn* in Boulogne). "Jugovichi," therefore, appears in our text rather than Yugovichi." The reader will find some other inconsistencies where we have been unable to devise a transliteration which was not unacceptably ugly.

The chief inconsistency, however, will appear to be our decision to leave the names of people and places in the Introduction entirely untransliterated. The introduction deals with so many historical figures and actual geographical places that we felt it best to spell the names in question with the conventional diacritical marks in order to facilitate easy reference should the reader wish to pursue one thing or another in historical, literary, or critical sources. Besides, rhythm and sound are not at issue here. The reader will understand that, for example, the Marko Kraljević of the Introduction is the Marko Kraljevich of the text. Although it is somewhat simplified, Subotić's key to pronunciation will help both with reading the Introduction and in making whatever transitions are less than obvious from spellings there to the partial

25

transliteration of the text. In addition to *lj* and *nj* cited above, Subotić lists: *c* like *ts* in lots; *ć* like *ch* in chalk; *č* like *ch* in church; *dž* like *j* in John; *s* like *sh* in ship; and *ž* like *s* in pleasure. All vowels, he reminds us, are pronounced "openly," as in Italian; and all are short. This may also be the place to note that Serbo-Croat permits the reversibility of Christian name and surname, and of name and title: Stefan Musich, for example, may also be called Musich Stefan; Marko Kraljevich may be called Kraljevich Marko. Either order is acceptable, although for some names and titles convention has established a preference: one should say Banovich Strahinja and not Strahinja Banovich. Finally, we have decided to spell Kosovo with a single *s* throughout, but we should note insistently again that all the vowels are short.

The Battle of Kosovo
Translated by
John Matthias and Vladeta Vučković

Fragment

Sultan Murad fell
                on level Kosovo!
And as he fell
                he wrote these few brief words,
Sent them to the castle
                at white Krushevats
To rest on Lazar's knees
                in his fine city.
"Lazar! Tsar!
                Lord of all the Serbs,
What has never been
                can never be:
One land only
                but two masters,
A single people
                who are doubly taxed;
We cannot both
                together rule here,
Therefore send me
                every tax and key,
Golden keys
                that unlock all the cities,
All the taxes
                for these seven years;
And if you do not send
                these things at once,
Bring your armies
                down to level Kosovo
And we'll divide the country
                with our swords . . . ."

When these words
                have come to Lazar's eyes
He sees them,
                weeping cruel tears.

The Downfall of the Kingdom of Serbia

Yes, and from Jerusalem,
>   O from that holy place,
A great gray bird,
>   a taloned falcon flew!
And in his beak
>   he held a gentle swallow.

But wait! it's not
>   a falcon, this gray bird,
It is a saint,
>   Holy Saint Elijah:
And he bears with him
>   no gentle swallow
But a letter
>   from the Blessed Mother.
He brings it
>   to the Tsar at Kosovo
And places it
>   upon his trembling knees.
And thus the letter itself
>   speaks to the Tsar:

"Lazar! Lazar!
>   Tsar of noble family,
Which kingdom is it
>   that you long for most?
Will you choose
>   a heavenly crown today?
Or will you choose
>   an earthly crown?
If you choose the earth
>   then saddle horses,
Tighten girths—
>   have your knights put on
Their swords and make
>   a dawn attack against

The Turks: your enemy
                will be destroyed.
But if you choose the skies
                then build a church—
O not of stone
                but out of silk and velvet—
Gather up your forces
                take the bread and wine,
For all shall perish,
                perish utterly,
And you, O Tsar,
                shall perish with them."

And when the Tsar
                has heard those holy words
He meditates,
                thinks every kind of thought:
"O Dearest God,
                what shall I do, and how?
Shall I choose the earth?
                Shall I choose
The skies?
                And if I choose the kingdom,
If I choose
                an earthly kingdom now,
Earthly kingdoms
                are such passing things—
A heavenly kingdom,
                raging in the dark,
                                endures eternally."

And Lazarus chose heaven,
                not the earth,
And tailored there
                a church at Kosovo—
O not of stone
                but out of silk and velvet—
And he summoned there
                the Patriarch of Serbia,
Summoned there
                the lordly twelve high bishops:

31

And he gathered up his forces,
                  had them
Take with him
                  the saving bread and wine.

As soon as Lazarus
                  has given out
His orders,
                  then across the level plain
Of Kosovo
                  pour all the Turks.

Supper in Krushevats

The Serbian Tsar
         will celebrate his Slava
Here in Krushevats,
         a well-protected fortress.
All the high nobility
         and all
The lesser lords
         he seats around the table—
All will honor now
         his holy patron saint.
On his right
         he places old Jug Bogdan
And next to him
         the nine brave Jugovichi.
On his left
         Vuk Brankovich sits down,
And then the other lords
         according to their rank.
Across from Lazarus
         is Captain Milosh;
And next to him
         are these two noble knights:
The first:
         Ivan Kosanchich,
And the second:
         Lord Milan Toplitsa.

Now the Tsar
         lifts up the golden goblet;
Lazarus thus questions
         all his lords:
"To whom, I ask you,
         shall I make this toast?
If I must toast old age—
         to old Jug Bogdan then;
If I must honor eminence—
         to Brankovich;

If I must trust emotion—
                     to the nine brave Jugovichi,
Sons of old Jug Bogdan,
                     brothers of my queen;
If I must bow to beauty—
                     to Ivan Kosanchich;
If I decide by height—
                     to tall Milan Toplitsa;
But if heroic courage
                     must decide me
I shall drink
                     to noble Captain Milosh.
Yes! to Milosh—
                     to nobody else at all.
I'll only toast the health
                     of Milosh Obilich.
Hail, Cousin!
                     friend of mine and traitor!
First of all my friend—
                     but finally my betrayer.
Tomorrow you'll betray me
                     on the field of Kosovo,
Escaping to
                     the Turkish Sultan, Murad!
So to your health,
                     dear Milosh, drink it up,
And keep the golden goblet
                     to remember Lazarus."

Then up on nimble legs
                     springs Milosh Obilich
And to the dark earth
                     bows himself and says:
"My thanks to you
                     O glorious Lazarus,
My thanks for that fine toast
                     and for your handsome gift,
But I can't thank you
                     for those words you spoke.
Let me die
                     if I should lie to you!

I have never been
                    unfaithful to my Tsar—
Never have I been
                    and never shall I be—
And I am sworn
                    to die for you at Kosovo,
For you
                    & for the Christian faith.
But Treason, Lazarus,
                    sits beside you now—
The traitor sips his wine
                    right up your sleeve.
It's Brankovich,
                    Vuk Brankovich I say!
And when on Vitus-day
                    tomorrow morning
We make our dawn attack
                    upon the Blackbirds' Field
We'll see right there
                    at bloody Kosovo
Who is loyal to you
                    and who is not!
I swear to you
                    in God Almighty's Name
That I shall go
                    at dawn to Kosovo
And slaughter like a pig
                    the Turkish Sultan,
Put my foot
                    upon his throat.
And then if God & good luck
                    aid me I'll return
For Brankovich
                    & bind him to my lance,
Bind him like the wool
                    around a distaff.
I'll drag him like that
                    back as far as Kosovo!"

Captain Milosh and
Ivan Kosanchich

And Milosh says
        to Ivan Kosanchich:
"My brother,
        have you seen the Turkish army?
Is it vast?
        and do we dare attack them?
Can we conquer Murad
        here at Kosovo?"

And Ivan Kosanchich
        answers him like this:
"My noble friend,
        O Milosh Obilich!
I have spied upon
        the Turkish army
And I tell you
        it is vast and strong.
If all the Serbs
        were changed to grains of salt
We could not even
        salt their wretched dinners!
For fully fifteen days
        I've walked among those hoards
And found there
        no beginning and no end.
From Mt. Mramor
        straight to Suvi Javor,
From Javor, brother,
        on to Sazlija,
From Sazlija
        across the Chemer Bridge,
From Chemer Bridge
        on to the town of Zvechan,
From Zvechan, Milosh,
        to the edge of Chechan,
And from Chechan
        to the mountain peaks—

Everywhere the Turks
                        line up in battle gear:
Horse is next to horse
                        and warriors all are massed.
Their lances are like
                        trunks of forest trees;
Their banners are like
                        endless sailing clouds
And all their tents are like
                        the drifting snows.
Ah! and if from heaven
                        a heavy rain should fall
Then not a single drop
                        would ever touch the earth
For all the Turks
                        and horses standing on it.
Turkish forces occupy
                        the field before us
Stretching
                        to the rivers Lab and Sitnitsa.
Sultan Murad's fallen
                        on the level plain of Mazgit!"

Then Milosh looks
                        at Kosanchich and asks:
"My brother,
                        tell me next where I can find
The tent
                        of mighty Sultan Murad
For I have sworn
                        to noble Lazarus
To slaughter like a pig
                        this foreign Tsar
And put my foot
                        upon his squealing throat."

And Ivan Kosanchich
                        replies like this:
"O Milosh Obilich,
                        I think you must be mad!

37

Where do you suppose
                    that tent is placed
But in the middle
                    of the vast encampment—
And even if you had
                    a falcon's wings
And flew down
                    from the clear blue skies above
Your wings would never
                    fly you out again alive!"

Then Milosh thus
                    implores Ivan to promise:
"O Ivan Kosanchich
                    my dearest brother—
Not in blood,
                    but so much like a brother—
Swear to me
                    not to tell the Tzar
What you have seen
                    and said to me just now.
Lazarus would
                    suffer anguish over it;
The army under him
                    would grow afraid.
We must both of us
                    say this instead:
Though the Turkish army
                    is not small,
We can easily
                    do battle with them
And defeat them . . .
                    This is what we've seen:
Not an army made of
                    knights and warriors
But of weary pilgrims,
                    old and crippled hodjas,
Artisans,
                    and skinny adolescents
Who have never
                    even tasted blood

And only come to Kosovo
            to see the world
Or earn a crust of bread,
            a cup of dark red wine . . .
And if there is
            a real Turkish army,
That one's fallen sick
            from dysentery
                        and has lost its way.
Far from here
            they shit upon the earth
In fear of us . . .
            and even all their horses
Suffer illnesses,
            ruined by distemper, laminitis,
Spreading fatal
            hoof and mouth disease
To captured cattle
            and to captured sheep."

Musich Stefan

In Maydan where
    they mine the purest silver
Musich Stefan drinks
    the dark red wine
That's brought to him
    by Vaistina his servant
To a table
    in his lordly castle.

When he has satisfied his thirst
    he says:
"Vaistina,
    my dearest friend and servant,
Drink and eat
    while I lie down to rest
And then go walk
    before our lordly castle:
Gaze into the clear
    transparent skies
And tell me:
    is the bright moon in the west?
Is the morning star
    rising in the east?
Has the hour arrived
    for us to journey
To the level plain
    of Kosovo
And join forces
    with the noble Tsar?
My son, you will remember
    that grave oath—
Lazarus exhorted us
    like this:
'Whoever is a Serb,
    of Serbian blood,
Whoever shares with me
    this heritage,
And he comes not
    to fight at Kosovo,

May he never have
                    the progeny
His heart desires,
                    neither son nor daughter;
Beneath his hand
                    let nothing decent grow—
Neither purple grapes
                    nor wholesome wheat;
Let him rust away
                    like dripping iron
Until his name
                    shall be extinguished!'"

Then Musich Stefan
                    rests upon soft pillows
While Vaistina his friend
                    and loyal servant
Eats his meal,
                    drinks his share of wine,
And goes to walk
                    before the lordly castle.
He looks into the clear
                    transparent skies
And sees the moon—
                    bright and in the west;
The morning star
                    is rising in the east.
The hour has thus arrived
                    for them to journey
To the level plain
                    of Kosovo
And join forces
                    with the noble Tsar.

Now Vaistina
                    takes horses from the stable—
Battle-horses,
                    one for each of them—
And saddles them,
                    arrays them beautifully.

Then he carries out
                    a noble silken banner
All embroidered
                    with twelve golden crosses
And a brilliant ikon
                    of Saint John,
Holy Patron Saint
                    of Musich Stefan.
He puts it down
                    before the castle keep
And climbs the stairs
                    to wake his master up.

Now as Vaistina
                    ascends those stairs
The wife of Musich Stefan
                    stops him there,
Embracing him.
                    Imploringly she says:
"O Servant Vaistina,
                    in Jesus' Name!
By God Almighty
                    and by Holy John,
Till now you were
                    my good & faithful friend.
If you are still my brother
                    then I beg you:
Do not awaken now
                    your sleeping master.
Pity me;
                    I've had an evil dream.
I dreamed I saw
                    a flock of doves in flight
with two gray falcons
                    flying on before them,
Flying right before
                    this very castle.
They flew to Kosovo
                    and landed there
In Sultan Murad's
                    cruel vast encampment—

But never did I see
                them rise again.
This, my brother,
                is a prophecy:
I fear that all of you
                are going to die."

Then Vaistina the servant
                speaks like this:
"Dearest sister,
                honored wife of Stefan!
I cannot, my sister,
                be unfaithful
To the master
                of this noble castle;
You are not bound
                as he and I are bound
By Lazarus's
                bitter exhortation:
I tell you truly—
                this is what he said:
'Whoever is a Serb,
                of Serbian blood,
Whoever shares with me
                this heritage,
And he comes not
                to fight at Kosovo,
May he never have
                the progeny
His heart desires,
                neither son nor daughter;
Beneath his hand
                let nothing decent grow—
Neither purple grapes
                nor wholesome wheat;
Let him rust away
                like dripping iron
Until his name
                shall be extinguished!'

43

Thus I cannot, sister,
                be unfaithful
To the master
                of this noble castle."

Then Vaistina goes up
                and wakes his master
Saying this:
                "The time is now upon us."
And Musich Stefan
                rises on strong legs
And washes slowly,
                puts on lordly garments.
He belts around his waist
                a well-forged saber,
Pours himself a glass
                of dark red wine
And toasts
                his holy patron saint,
And then a quick
                and providential journey,
And last of all
                the saving cross of Jesus.
All this in his castle
                at his banquet table—
Where Stefan will not
                eat or drink again.

Then they walk
                before the lordly castle,
Mount their ready
                chestnut battle-horses
And unfurl
                the cross-embroidered banner.
Drums and trumpets
                break the morning silence—
Off they ride to battle
                in the name of God!

When the brilliant dawn
                    has cast its light upon them
Over Kosovo,
                    that flat and graceful plain,
There suddenly appears
                    a lovely maiden
Bearing in her hands
                    two empty golden goblets.
Beneath her arm
                    she has a noble helmet
Made of wound white silk
                    with feathers intertwined
Which are worked
                    in silver at their ends
And sewn with precious
                    threads of yellow gold—
And all embroidered
                    at the top with pearls.
Then Musich Stefan
                    speaks to her like this:
"May God Almighty
                    bless you and be with you—
But where can you
                    have found that noble helmet?
Were you yourself
                    upon the field of battle?
Give it to me,
                    dear one, for a moment,
For I will know at once
                    which hero wore it.
I promise by my
                    providential journey
That I will never
                    injure or betray you."

The lovely maiden
                    answered him and said:
"Greetings to you,
                    warrior of the Tsar!
I was not myself
                    upon the field of battle

45

But my mother woke me
                    early to get water
From the river Sitnitsa
                    that flows nearby
And when I got there—
                    what a flood I saw!
Of muddy water,
                    horses, dying heroes,
Turkish calpacs,
                    fezes, bloody turbans,
And the helmets
                    worn by noble Serbs
Made of wound white silk
                    with feathers intertwined.
I saw this helmet
                    floating near the bank
And waded out a bit
                    to reach it there.
I have at home
                    a little younger brother
And I wanted him
                    to have it for a present.
Besides, I'm young myself;
                    I like the feathers on it."

She gives the helmet
                    to the mounted knight.
As soon as Stefan
                    has it in his hands
He recognizes it
                    and starts to weep;
Tears flow down
                    his stern & noble face.
He slaps his side
                    so fiercely that he breaks
A golden cuff link
                    joining his right sleeves
And tears the velvet
                    of his trouser leg.

"May God in heaven
                help me and protect me!
Now the curse of Lazar
                surely falls!"
And he returns
                the helmet to the girl
And reaches in his
                pocket with his hand
And gives three golden
                ducats to her, saying:
"Take them, dear one,
                lovely Maid of Kosovo,
For I am going
                into battle now
To fight the Turks
                in Jesus' Holy Name.
If God allows me
                to return alive
I'll have for you
                a better gift by far—
But if, my sister,
                I should die in battle,
Remember me by these
                three golden ducats."

Then they spurred
                their horses into battle
Across the flooding
                muddy river Sitnitsa
And rode into
                the camp of Sultan Murad.
Musich Stefan fought
                and killed three pashas,
But when he met the fourth
                that warrior smote him—
And there he died
                beside his Servant Vaistina
And with his army
                of twelve thousand souls.

Great Tsar Lazar
                also perished on that day
And with him died
                a good and ancient Empire—
With him died
                the Kingdom of this Earth.

Tsar Lazar and
Tsaritsa Militsa

Now when at Krushevats
        the Tsar is camped
And takes his supper
        on the eve of battle
Militsa his Queen
        implores him thus:
"O Lazar,
        Golden Crown of Serbia,
You ride tomorrow
        out to Kosovo
And take away your
        servants & your knights;
You leave me no one
        at the castle, Sire,
Who'd ride out with
        a letter to the field
Of Kosovo and bring
        an answer back.
You take away with you
        my nine dear brothers;
All the Jugovichi
        ride with you.
I ask you this:
        leave but one behind.
Leave me just one
        brother here to swear by."

And Lazarus thus speaks
        to her and says:
"My Lady Militsa,
        my dear Tsaritsa—
Which brother is it
        you would like for me
To leave with you
        in this white castle tower?"
And she:—
        "Give me Boshko Jugovich!"

And he, noble Prince
                      of all the Serbs:
"My Lady Militsa,
                      my dear Tsaritsa,
Tomorrow when
                      the white day brightly dawns,
When the day dawns,
                      the sun bright in the east,
And when the portals
                      of the town are opened,
Go and stand
                      beside those city gates
For there will pass
                      the army in its ranks
And all the horsemen
                      with their battle-lances.
Boshko Jugovich
                      will lead them all
And carry high
                      the cross-emblazoned banner.
Give him all
                      my blessings and say this:
That he shall give
                      the flag to someone else
And stay with you
                      in this white castle tower."
When dawn has broken
                      early in the morning
And the portals
                      of the town are opened
Out she walks,
                      Lazarus's queen,
And goes to stand
                      beside the city gate
Where all the army
                      passes by in ranks.
Out before the warriors
                      with their lances
Comes her brother,
                      Boshko Jugovich,
Riding in his
                      noble golden armor

On his golden-harnessed
                   battle stallion
Holding high
                   the cross-emblazoned banner
Which envelops him,
                   my brothers, to the waist.
On the staff
                   there is a golden apple,
And on the apple
                   golden crosses stand
From which there hang
                   several golden tassels
Dangling in the breeze
                   about his shoulders.
Now Tsaritsa Militsa
                   goes up to him
And takes his horse's
                   bridle in her hand.
She puts her arms
                   around her brother's neck
And thus she softly
                   speaks to him and says:
"O my brother,
                   Boshko Jugovich,
Lazarus has given
                   you to me
And tells you
                   not to go to Kosovo;
He sends his blessing
                   to you and he says:
To give your flag
                   to anyone you like
And stay with me
                   at white-walled Krushevats
That I will have
                   a brother here to swear by."

Boshko Jugovich
                   then speaks like this:
"Go back, my sister,
                   to your castle tower.

It is not for me
          to go with you
Or give away
          this banner that I hold
Even if the Tsar
          would give me Krushevats;
What would all
          my comrades say of me?
Look upon this
          coward Jugovich!
The one who dares not
          go to Kosovo
And spill his blood
          for Jesus' Holy Cross
And for his faith
          to die upon that plain."
With that he spurs
          his horse on through the gate.

And next rides out
          Jug Bogdan, Boshko's father,
And behind him
          seven Jugovichi;
One by one she stops
          them and implores them
But not a one
          would even look at her.
She waits in misery
          beside the portals
Until her brother
          Voin comes riding past
Leading close behind him
          Lazar's horses
All caparisoned
          with golden trappings.
She stops his chestnut,
          takes it by the bridle,
And then she throws
          her arms around her brother.
Thus she softly
          speaks to him and says:

"O Voin Jugovich,
                    my dearest brother,
Lazar gives you
                    to me for a present!
He sends his blessing
                    to you and he says:
Give to someone else
                    those noble horses
And stay with me
                    at white-walled Krushevats
That I will have
                    a brother here to swear by."
Her brother Voin
                    thus answers her and says:
"Go back, my sister,
                    to your castle tower—
For as a warrior
                    I may not return,
Nor would I leave
                    these horses of the Tsar
Even if I knew
                    that I would perish.
I ride out to
                    the level field of Kosovo
To spill my blood
                    for Jesus' Holy Cross
And die with all
                    my brothers for the faith."
With that he spurs
                    his horse on through the gate.
When Lady Militsa
                    has seen all this
She falls down fainting
                    on the cold hard stone
And lies unconscious,
                    still as if in death.
Glorious Lazar,
                    Prince of all the Serbs,
Is next to pass,
                    and when he sees his queen
He weeps, and tears
                    flow down his cheeks.

52

He looks around him
                    turns to left and right,
And calls out to
                    his servant Goluban:
"Goluban, my dear
                    and faithful servant,
Dismount at once
                    from your white horse
And take my lady
                    in your strong white arms
And carry her
                    into the narrow tower.
I free you before God
                    from your grave oath.
Do not ride out
                    to fight at Kosovo
But stay with her
                    inside the castle tower."

When Goluban has heard
                    his master's words
He weeps, and tears
                    flow down his cheeks;
As ordered he dismounts
                    from his white horse
And lifts the lady up
                    in his white arms
And carries her
                    into the castle tower.
But yet his heart
                    torments him: he must go
And ride to battle
                    on the Blackbirds' Field.
Turning back at once
                    to his white horse
He mounts
                    and rides to level Kosovo.

As in the east
                    the morning brightly dawns
Two black ravens
                    fly to Krushevats
From Kosovo,
                    that wide and level plain,

And land upon
　　　　the narrow castle tower,
The castle tower
　　　　of Lazarus the Tsar.
The first bird caws,
　　　　the second starts to talk:
"Is this the tower
　　　　of Glorious Lazarus,
Or is there no one
　　　　home in this white castle?"
Only Lady Militsa
　　　　is there to hear,
And she alone walks
　　　　out before the tower.
Thus she speaks
　　　　and asks the two black birds:
"Ravens! in the name
　　　　of God Almighty
Tell me where you
　　　　come from this bright morning.
Could it be
　　　　you come from Kosovo?
Have you seen
　　　　two mighty armies there?
And did those armies
　　　　join in furious combat?
Great black birds:
　　　　which army won the battle?"
Then the ravens
　　　　answered, both together:
"In the name of God,
　　　　Tsaritsa Militsa,
We come today
　　　　from level Kosovo,
And we have seen
　　　　two mighty armies there;
Those armies met
　　　　in battle yesterday
And both the Tsar
　　　　and Sultan have been slain.

Among the Turks
                    some few are left alive,
But fewer still
                    among the Serbs yet breathe,
And all of them
                    have cruel bleeding wounds."

Even as the ravens
                    speak those words
The Servant Milutin
                    comes riding up:
His own right arm
                    he bears in his left hand;
Bleeding from his
                    seventeen grave wounds,
He reins his sweating
                    blood-drenched war-horse in.
Lady Militsa
                    thus questions him:
"What happened to you
                    Servant Milutin?
Did you abandon
                    Lazar on the field?"
And Servant Milutin
                    replies to her:
"Help me down,
                    dear lady, from my horse,
And bathe with cool
                    water all my wounds;
Quench my thirst
                    with red reviving wine;
These evil wounds
                    will be the end of me."
The Lady Militsa
                    takes him gently down
And bathes his wounds
                    with cool water there,
And gives him dark red wine
                    to quench his thirst.
When she has thus
                    attended to his needs
She questions
                    him again & softly asks:

55

"What happened,
                Milutin, at Kosovo?
The noble Tsar
                & old Jug Bogdan— dead?
The Jugovichi,
                nine of them, all dead?
Vuk Brankovich
                and great Lord Milosh— dead?
And Strahinja the Ban
                beside them all?"
The wounded servant
                answers her and says:
"All remain,
                my lady, on the field
Where the glorious Tsar
                has bravely perished.
There are many
                broken lances there
Belonging both to Turks
                and noble Serbs—
But many more of ours
                have broken, Lady,
Than the Turks'
                defending Lazarus,
Fighting for our
                glorious Lord and Master.
And old Jug Bogdan,
                Lady, lost his life
At the beginning,
                in the dawn attack
Along with his
                eight sons, the Jugovichi,
Where brother fought
                by brother to the end
As long as he
                could strike and cut;
But Boshko Jugovich
                remains there still,
His cross-emblazoned
                banner waving high,
Where he chases
                Turks in frightened herds

As a hunting falcon
            chases doves.
And Strahinja died too
            where blood rose to the knees,
While Milosh, Lady,
            lost his noble life
Fighting near
            the river Sitnitsa
Where many dying
            Turks lie all around.
But Milosh killed
            the Turkish Sultan, Murad,
And slaughtered many
            Turkish soldiers with him.
May God Almighty
            bless the one who bore him!
He leaves immortal fame
            to all the Serbs
To be forever told
            in song and story
As long as Kosovo
            and human kind endure.
But ask me nothing
            of Vuk Brankovich!
May the one who gave
            him birth be damned!
Cursed be his tribe
            and his posterity,
For he betrayed
            the Tsar at Kosovo,
And led away twelve
            thousand men, my Lady,
Led his knights away
            with him from Kosovo."

Tsaritsa Militsa and Vladeta the Voyvoda

Tsaritsa Militsa

   went out to walk
Before the castle

   at white Krushevats,
And with her there

   were her two daughters:
Vukosava

   and the pretty Mara.
Then up to them

   came Vladeta the Voyvoda
Riding on a bay

   a charging war-horse;
Vladeta had forced

   the horse into a sweat
And it was bathed

   all over in white foam.
Tsaritsa Militsa

   spoke to him and said:
"In the name of God

   good knight of the Tsar,
Why have you

   so forced your horse to sweat?
Aren't you coming

   from the field of Kosovo?
Did you see

   great Lazar riding there?
Did you see

   my master and your own?"
And Vladeta

   responded in his turn:
"In the name of God

   Tsaritsa Militsa,
I have ridden

   from the level field,
But I fear

   I did not see the Tsar.
I saw his war-horse

   chased by many Turks,

58

And thus I think
                    our noble Lord is dead."
When Tsaritsa Militsa
                    had heard that news
She wept
                    and tears ran down her face.
And then she looked
                    at Vladeta and asked:
"Tell me more
                    good knight of the Tsar,
When you were on
                    that wide and level plain,
Did you see my father
                    and my noble brothers there?
Did you see the Jugovichi
                    and Jug Bogdan?"
And Vladeta
                    thus answered her and said:
"As I rode out
                    and over level Kosovo
I saw the Jugovichi,
                    nine of them, your brothers,
And I saw your father,
                    old Jug Bogdan, there:
They were in the midst
                    of all the fighting
And their arms were bloody
                    clear up to their shoulders,
Their tempered swords
                    clear up to the hilts;
How their arms
                    grew weary though and sank
Struggling with the Turks
                    out on that field!"

Again the wife of Lazar
                    spoke to him and said:
"Voyvoda
                    stay with me and wait!
Did you see
                    the husbands of my daughters?

Did you see
           Vuk Brankovich and Milosh?"
And Vladeta
           the Voyvoda replied:
"I have gone all over
           level Kosovo,
And I have seen
           what I have seen.
I did see Captain Milosh,
           Milosh Obilich,
And he was standing
           on that level field;
I saw him lean
           upon his battle lance
And saw
           that it was broken
And the Turks
           were swarming on him
Until now, I think,
           he surely must have died.
And did I see
           Vuk Brankovich at all?
I did not see him—
           let the sun not see him either!
For he betrayed the Tsar
           out on that field,
The noble Tsar,
           your master and my own."

The Kosovo Maiden

On a Sunday
                early in the morning
The Maid of Kosovo
                awoke to brilliant sun
And rolled her sleeves
                above her snow-white elbows;

On her back she carries
                warm, white bread,
And in her hands she bears
                two golden goblets,
one of water,
                one of dark red wine.
Seeking out
                the plain of Kosovo,
She walks upon the field
                of slaughter there
Where noble Lazarus,
                the Tsar, was slain,
And turns the warriors
                over in their blood;
Should one still breathe
                she bathes him with the water
And offers him,
                as if in sacrament,
The dark red wine to drink,
                the bread to eat.

At length she comes
                to Pavle Orlovich,
Standard-bearer
                of his lord the Tsar,
And finds him still alive,
                though torn and maimed:
His right hand and his
                left leg are cut off
And his handsome chest
                is crushed and broken

So that she can see
                his lungs inside.
She moves him from
                the pool of blood
And bathes his wounds
                with clear and cool water;
She offers him,
                as if in sacrament,
The dark red wine to drink,
                the bread to eat.

When she has thus
                attended to his needs,
Pavle Orlovich
                revives and speaks:
"Maid of Kosovo,
                my dearest sister,
What misfortune
                leads you to this plain
To turn the warriors
                over in their blood?
Whom can you be
                looking for out here?
Have you lost
                a brother or a nephew?
Have you lost perhaps
                an aging father?"
And the Maid
                of Kosovo replies:
"O my brother,
                O my unknown hero!
It is not for
                someone of my blood
I'm searching:
                not an aging father;
Neither is it for
                a brother or a nephew.
Do you remember,
                brave and unknown warrior,
When Lazar gave
                communion to his army

With the help
                of thirty holy monks
Near the lovely
                church of Samodrezha
And it took them
                twenty days to do it?
All the Serbian army
                took communion.
At the end there came
                three warrior Lords:
The first was
                captain Milosh Obilich,
The next was
                Ivan Kosanchich,
And the last the warrior
                Milan Toplitsa.
It happened that
                I stood beside the gates
As Milosh Obilich
                passed grandly by—
There is no fairer
                warrior in this world—
He trailed his saber
                there upon the stones
And on his head he wore
                a helmet made
Of wound white silk
                with feathers intertwined
A brightly colored cloak
                hung down his back
And round his neck
                he wore a silken scarf.
As he passed he turned
                and looked at me
And offered me his
                brightly colored cloak,
Took it off and gave
                it to me, saying:
'Maiden, take this
                brightly colored cloak
By which I hope
                you will remember me—

This cloak by which
          you can recall my name:
Dear soul, I'm going
          out to risk my life
In battle for
          the great Tsar Lazarus;
Pray God, my love,
          that I return alive,
And that good fortune
          shortly shall be yours:
I will give you
          as a bride to Milan,
Milan Toplitsa,
          my sworn blood-brother,
Noble Milan who
          became my brother
Before God Almighty
          and Saint John:
To him I'll give you
          as a virgin bride.'

After him rode
          Ivan Kosanchich—
There is no fairer
          warrior in this world.
He trailed his saber
          there upon the stones
And on his head he wore
          a helmet made
Of wound white silk
          with feathers intertwined,
A brightly colored cloak
          hung down his back
While round his neck
          he wore a silken scarf
And on his hand
          he had a golden ring.
As he passed he turned
          and looked at me
And offered me
          the glowing golden ring,
Took it off and gave
          it to me saying:

64

'Maiden, take this
        golden wedding ring
By which I hope
        you will remember me—
This ring by which
        you can recall my name:
Dear soul, I'm going
        out to risk my life
In battle for
        the great Tsar Lazarus;
Pray God, my love,
        that I return alive,
And that good fortune
        shortly shall be yours:
I will give you
        as a bride to Milan,
Milan Toplitsa,
        my sworn blood-brother,
Noble Milan who
        became my brother
Before God Almighty
        and Saint John:
I will be the best man
        at your wedding.'

After him rode
        Milan Toplitsa—
There is no fairer
        warrior in this world.
He trailed his saber
        there upon the stones
And on his head he wore
        a helmet made
Of wound white silk
        with feathers intertwined;
A brightly colored cloak
        hung down his back
While round his neck
        he wore a silken scarf
And on his wrist
        he had a golden torque.

As he passed he turned
                    and looked at me
And offered me
                    the shining golden torque,
Took it off and
                    gave it to me, saying:
'Maiden, take this
                    shining golden torque
By which I hope
                    you will remember me—
This torque by which
                    you can recall my name:
Dear soul, I'm going
                    out to risk my life
In battle for
                    the great Tsar Lazarus;
Pray God, my love,
                    that I return alive,
And that good fortune
                    shortly shall be yours
And I will take you
                    for my faithful wife.'
With that the warrior Lords
                    all rode away—
And so I search upon
                    this field of slaughter."

Pavle Orlovich
                    then spoke and said:
"O my dearest sister,
                    Maid of Kosovo!
Do you see, dear soul,
                    those battle-lances
Where they're piled
                    the highest over there?
That is where the blood
                    of heroes flowed
In pools higher than
                    the flanks of horses,

Higher even than
                the horses' saddles—
right up to the riders'
                silken waistbands.
Those you came to find
                have fallen there;
Go back, maiden, to your
                white-walled dwelling.
Do not stain your skirt
                and sleeves with blood."

When she has heard
                the wounded hero's words
She weeps, and tears
                flow down her pale face;
She leaves the plain
                of Kosovo and walks
To her white village
                wailing, crying out:—
"O pity, pity!
                I am cursed so utterly
That if I touched
                a greenly leafing tree
it would dry and wither,
                blighted and defiled."

Fragment

"Who is that fine hero,
                    who's the one
Sweeping with
                    his tempered sword,
His tempered sword
                    in his right hand,
To cut off
                    twenty heads?"
"That is
                    Banovich Strahinja!"

"Who is that fine hero,
                    who's the one,
Impaling four
                    before he's done
Upon his lance
                    and heaving them
Behind him
                    in the river Sitnitsa?"
"That is
                    Srdja Zlopogledja!"

"Who is that fine hero,
                    who's the one,
Riding on
                    the great white stallion,
Holding high
                    the banner in his hands,
Chasing Turks
                    around in bands
And plunging them
                    into the river Sitnitsa?"
"That is
                    Boshko Jugovich!"

The Death of the Mother
of the Jugovichi

Dear God! How great
　　　　　　the wonder of it all—
When the army fell
　　　　　　on level Kosovo
With all the Jugovichi
　　　　　　in its ranks—
Nine brave brothers
　　　　　　and the tenth, their father!

The mother
　　　　　　of the Jugovichi prays
That God will give her
　　　　　　quick eyes of a falcon
And a swan's white wings
　　　　　　that she might fly
Out over Kosovo,
　　　　　　that level plain,
And see the Jugovichi—
　　　　　　all nine brothers
And their father,
　　　　　　noble old Jug Bogdan.

And God Almighty
　　　　　　grants her what she asks—
Eyes of a falcon,
　　　　　　white wings of a swan—
And out she flies
　　　　　　over level Kosovo
And finds the Jugovichi
　　　　　　lying slain—
All nine brothers,
　　　　　　and the tenth, Jug Bogdan.

Driven in the ground
　　　　　　nine lances stand
With nine gray falcons
　　　　　　perching on their ends;

Beside the lances
                    nine brave horses wait,
And near the horses
                    nine grim rampant lions.
She hears the horses
                    neigh, the lions roar,
The nine gray falcons
                    scream and croak and caw,
And still her heart
                    is cold as any stone
And no tears rise at all,
                    and no tears fall.

Then she takes with her
                    the nine brave horses,
And she takes with her
                    the rampant lions,
And she takes with her
                    the nine gray falcons—
Slowly leads them off
                    to her white castle.

From far away her sons'
                    nine wives could see her—
And out they walk
                    before the castle tower:
And as the mother hears
                    the widows weeping
She hears the horses
                    neigh, the lions roar,
The nine gray falcons
                    scream and croak and caw.
And still her heart
                    is cold as any stone
And no tears rise at all,
                    and no tears fall.

When it is very late,
                    when it is midnight,
Damian's gray horse
                    begins to scream;

70

The mother goes
        to Damian's wife and asks:
"O dearest daughter,
        my son's beloved wife,
Why does Damian's
        stallion scream like this?
Is he hungry for
        the choicest wheat?
Does he thirst for
        cool Zvechan waters?"
And the wife of Damian
        answers her:
"O my mother,
        mother of my Damian,
The stallion does not
        scream for choicest wheat,
Neither does he thirst
        for Zvechen waters;
Damian used to feed him
        oats till midnight,
And at midnight
        he would ride the roads;
The horse is grieving
        for his noble master—
That he did not bring
        him here upon his back."
And still the mother's heart
        is cold as any stone,
And no tears rise at all,
        and no tears fall.

When dawn has broken
        early in the morning,
Two black ravens
        fly up to the castle,
Their wings all red
        and bloody to the shoulders
And their beaks
        all foaming with white foam.

They carry there
                    a warrior's severed hand
With a wedding ring
                    upon its finger
And they drop it
                    in the mother's lap.
The mother of the
                    Jugovichi takes the hand
And stares at it,
                    turns it in her lap,
And then she calls
                    to Damian's faithful wife:
"O my daughter,
                    beloved wife of Damian,
Do you know
                    whose severed hand this is?"
And the wife of Damian
                    answers her:
"O dearest Lady,
                    mother of my husband,
This is the hand
                    of Damian, your son;
I know because
                    I recognize this ring
Which is the ring
                    I gave him at our wedding."
Again the mother
                    takes the severed hand
And stares at it,
                    turns it in her lap:
Softly then she speaks
                    to that white hand:

"O dear dead hand,
                    O dear unripe green apple,
Where did you grow,
                    where were you torn away?
Dear God! you grew
                    upon this mother's lap
And you were torn away
                    upon the plain of Kosovo!"

And now the mother
                    can endure no more
And so her heart
                    swells and breaks with sorrow
For the Jugovichi—
                    all nine brothers
And the tenth of them,
                    Jug Bogdan.

The Miracle of
Lazar's Head

When they cut off Lazar's head
              upon the Blackbirds' Field
Not a single Serb
              was there to see it.
But it happened
              that a Turkish boy saw,
A slave,
              the son of one who had been made
Herself a slave,
              a Serbian mother.
Thus the boy spoke
              having seen it all:
"Oh have pity, brothers;
              Oh have pity, Turks.
Here before us lies
              a sovereign's noble head!
In God's name
              it would be a sin
If it were pecked at
              by the eagles and the crows
Or trampled on
              by horses and by heroes."
He took the head
              of holy Lazar then
And covered it
              and put it in a sack
And carried it
              until he found a spring
And put the head
              into the waters there.
For forty years
              the head lay in that spring
While the body lay
              upon the field at Kosovo.

It was not pecked
                by eagles or by crows.
It was not trampled on
                by horses or by heroes.
For that, Dear Lord,
                all thanks be to Thee.

Then one day
                there came from lovely Skoplje
A group of youthful carters
                who conveyed
Bulgarians and Greeks
                to Vidin and to Nish
And stopped to spend the night
                at Kosovo.
They made a dinner
                on that level field,
And ate
                and then grew thirsty afterwards.
They lit the candle
                in their lantern then
And went to look
                for waters of a spring.
Then it was
                that one young carter said:
"See the brilliant moonlight
                in the water there."
The second carter
                answered him:
"My brother,
                I don't think it's moonlight,"
While the third
                was silent, saying nothing,
Turning in his silence
                to the east,
And all at once
                calling out to God,
The one true God,
                and holy sainted Nicholas:
"Help me God!
                Help me holy Nicholas!"

He plunged
                        into the waters of the spring
And lifted out
                        into the quiet air
The holy head of Lazar,
                        Tsar of all the Serbs.
He placed it on
                        the green grass by the spring
And turned to get
                        some water in a jug
So the thirsty carters
                        all could drink.
When next they looked
                        upon the fertile earth
The head no longer
                        rested on the grass
But rolled out all alone
                        across the level field,
The holy head
                        moving towards the body
To join it
                        the way it was before.

When in the morning
                        bright day dawned
The three young carters
                        sent the tidings off—
A message to
                        the holy Christian priests
Which summoned some
                        three hundred of them there
And summoned bishops,
                        twelve of them,
And summoned
                        four old patriarchs
From Pech, Constantinople,
                        and Jerusalem.
They all put on
                        their holy vestments then,
Put on their heads
                        the tall peaked caps of monks,

And took into their hands
                    the ancient chronicles,
And read out prayers,
                    and kept long vigils there
For three long days
                    and three dark nights,
Neither sitting down
                    nor seeking any rest,
Neither lying down
                    nor ever sleeping,
But questioning the saint
                    and asking him
To which great church
                    or monastery he would go:
Whether Opovo
                    or Krushedol,
Whether Jaska
                    or Beshenovo,
Whether Rakovats
                    or Shishatovats
Whether Djivsha
                    or Kuvezhdin
Or whether he would
                    rather go to Macedonia.
But the saint
                    would go to none of these,
And wished to stay
                    at lovely Ravanitsa,
The church he had
                    himself endowed
Which rose below
                    the mountain of Kuchaj—
His own church,
                    the one he built himself,
Built with his own bread,
                    with his own treasure,
And not with tears
                    wept by wretched subjects,
In those years
                    he walked upon this earth.

The Death of
Duke Prijezda

Message after message
              after message:
Who is sending them?
              Just who are they for?
The Turkish Sultan Mehmed
              sends them all
And they are for Prijezda,
              Duke of Stalach;
They come to him
              in his white castle there.

"O Prijezda,
              noble Voyvoda of Stalach,
I demand you send me
              your three treasures:
First,
              your deadly tempered sword
That cuts so easily
              through wood and stone,
Through wood and stone
              and even through cold iron;
Second, send
              your gallant war-horse, Zhdral,
That flies across
              the wide and level fields
And leaps the height
              of double rampart walls;
Third, I want
              your faithful wife."

Duke Prijezda
              studies what he reads,
Studies it
              and writes a short reply:
"Sultan Mehmed,
              Tsar of all the Turks,
Raise as large an army
              as you like

And come to Stalach
                any time you choose.
Whatever way
                you may attack us here,
I will not give you
                any of my treasures;
For myself alone
                I forged my sword,
For myself alone
                I fed my gallant Zhdral,
And for myself alone
                I took a wife:
I will not give you
                any of my treasures."
The Turkish Sultan Mehmed
                raised an army then,
Raised an army,
                led it off to Stalach;
He bombarded Stalach
                three long years,
But not a single stone
                did he dislodge;
He found no way
                to conquer that white city,
Nor would he end the seige
                and march back home.

One fine morning
                on a Saturday
Duke Prijezda's wife
                climbed slowly up
The rampart walls
                surrounding little Stalach
And from those heights
                she gazed into the Morava,
The muddy river
                down below the city.
Prijezda's wife
                thus spoke to him and said:
"O Prijezda,
                O my dearest master,

I'm afraid,

           my master and my lord,
The Turks will blow us up

           from underground!"
Duke Prijezda

           answered her and said:
"Be silent, love,

           do not talk like that.
How can anybody

           tunnel under Morava?"
After that

           Sunday morning dawned,
And all the nobles

           went into the church
To stand and hear

           the solemn mass of God;
And when they left the church

           and came back out
Duke Prijezda

           spoke to them and said:
"My Lords,

           my powerful right wings,
My wings by which I fly

           to eat and drink and fight,
After we have eaten

           and have drunk our wine,
Let us open up

           the castle gates
And make a flying raid

           against the Turks,
Letting God and fortune

           give us what they want!"
Thus Prijezda

           calls out to his wife:
"My love, go down

           into the castle cellar
And bring us up

           the brandy and the wine."
Jelitsa then took

           two golden pitchers
And went below

           into the castle cellar,

But when she reached
                    the bottom of the stairs,
She saw the place
                    was full of Turkish soldiers
Drinking cool wine
                    out of their boots
And toasting first
                    the health of Lady Jelitsa
And then her husband's death,
                    the death of Duke Prijezda.
She dropped her pitchers
                    on the cellar stones
And ran upstairs
                    into the castle hall.
"Your wine is bad,
                    my lord and master,
Very bad,
                    your brandy is worse still!
The castle cellar's full
                    of Turkish soldiers
Drinking cool wine
                    out of their boots.
First they drink my health
                    and then they drink to you,
But you—
                    they bury you alive,
They bury you
                    and then drink to your soul."
Duke Prijezda
                    then leapt to his feet
And opened up
                    the portals of the town;
They made a sortie
                    out against the Turks,
And closed with them
                    and dueled with them there
Until some sixty
                    of the lords were dead,
Sixty lords,
                    but thousands of the Turks;
After that
                    Prijezda rode back home

And locked the city gates
                    against the Turks.
He took his deadly sword
                    out of its sheath
And cut the head off Zhdral,
                    his gallant war-horse:
"Zhdral, Zhdral,
                    O my precious dear,
The Turkish Tsar
                    will not ride on your back."
Then he broke
                    his sharp and tempered sword:
"O tempered sword,
                    O my true right hand,
The Turkish Tsar
                    must never belt you on!"
Then he sought
                    his lady in the castle
And he took his lady
                    gently by the hand:
"Dearest Jelitsa,
                    wise and faithful lady,
Will you choose
                    to die with me today
Or will you be
                    the lover of a Turk?"
The Lady Jelitsa
                    shed many tears:
"In honor I will
                    die with you today;
I will not be
                    the lover of a Turk
Or trample on
                    the honorable cross;
They cannot force me
                    to betray my faith."
Then they joined hands,
                    the two of them,
And went up on the ramparts
                    above Stalach;
There it was
                    that Jelitsa thus spoke:

"O Prijezda,
                    O my dearest master,
The waters of the Morava
                    have nursed us;
The waters of the Morava
                    should bury us!"
And holding hands
                    they leapt into the river.

Sultan Mehmed
                    finally conquered Stalach,
But he did not obtain
                    a single treasure.
Bitterly he cursed,
                    this Turkish Tsar:
"May God destroy you,
                    O Stalach castle!
I had three thousand men
                    when I arrived;
Now I start for home
                    with just five hundred!"

Marko Kraljevich and the Eagle

Marko lies beside
          the high road of the Tsar,
His spear behind his head,
          planted in the earth:
He draws around him there
          his dark green dolman,
Covers up his face
          with silver-threaded cloth.
Sharats stands beside him,
          tethered to the spear-shaft—
And on the top of it
          there perches a great eagle.
He spreads his wings,
          making shade for Marko,
And gives him cool water
          from his beak,
Cool water
          for the wounded hero.

But suddenly a Vila
          cries out from the woods:
"In God's name
          great gray eagle there,
Whatever kind of goodness
          did this Marko do for you,
What act of kindness
          or of charity
That you should stretch your wings
          and shade him in this way
And bring him water
          in your beak,
Cool water
          for the wounded hero?"

And now the bird, the eagle,
                    speaks to him and says:
"Silence, Vila!
                    Shut your stupid mouth!
What sort of goodness has
                    this Marko *failed* to do,
What act of charity
                    has he *not* done for me?
It could be even you
                    remember this—
The army dropping off
                    like flies at Kosovo,
The two Tsars
                    dying on the field—
Murad dying,
                    great Tsar Lazar dying—
And all the blood
                    rising to the stirrups,
Rising even to the
                    silken belts of heroes,
Men and horses
                    floating in it, swimming,
Horse by horse
                    & hero next to hero—
And then the coming
                    of the hungry birds.

As we ate our fill
                    of human flesh
And drank our fill
                    of human blood
My wings grew wet
                    and sticky in the sun
Which burst out flaming
                    in the crystal sky
And suddenly
                    I could not fly at all
So stiff with blood
                    & scorched had grown my wings.
When all the other birds
                    had flown away

I alone remained
                    on level Kosovo
Trampled under foot
                    by horses and by heroes.

Then God sent Marko
                    to me on that plain
Who plucked me from
                    the flowing blood of heroes
And set me down behind him
                    on the back of Sharats.
He took me straight
                    into the nearest woods
And put me on
                    the green branch of a pine.
Then a gentle rain
                    began to rain.
It fell down from the sky
                    and washed my wings,
Washed away the blood
                    of noble heroes,
And I could fly above
                    beyond the forest
And join all the eagles,
                    join my swift companions.

To V.V.:
On Our Translations
of the Kosovo Fragments

Vladeta the Voyvoda!
                    knight who brings the news
From Kosovo
                    to gracious Militsa,
Lazarus's queen,
                    sister of the Jugovichi,
Daughter of Jug Bogdan—
                    that's the stock you're made of!
In the name
                    of God Almighty
As they all repeat
                    in these old epic poems
We struggle with
                    (and even in the name
Of Allah maybe)
                    what could ever bring
A hero and a Serb
                    To South Bend, Indiana?

Where Ivan Mestrovich
                    petered out his talent
In the awful portrait busts
                    and bland madonnas
Of his exile
                    we meet beside
The only decent
                    piece of work in town—
His *Jacob's Well*
                    and puzzle over
Fates as dark
                    as those of Lazarus
And Milosh Obilich
                    sung down centuries
Of Turkish occupation
                    by dusty peasant guslars
Who didn't need to know
                    that fancy alphabet
Saint Cyril left behind
                    in which reforming Vuk
Spelled out phonetically
                    a living language

89

Where one itches through
　　　　　the final syllables of names
And scratches at the surface
　　　　　of a destiny
In verbal fragments
　　　　　of a people's epic past.

How unlikely, Vladeta,
　　　　　that we should meet at all.
In 1941 when I was born
　　　　　beside a silly field
Of vegetables
　　　　　that noncombatant types
Were urged to cultivate—
　　　　　officially they called
Such doubtful husbandry
　　　　　a "Victory Garden"—
You at just eighteen
　　　　　had taken to the hills
With Tito's Partisans
　　　　　where every urgent message
Sent to Stalin
　　　　　(later on to Churchill)
Was the same:
　　　　　More Boots!
The rugged karst
　　　　　that cut away your soles
Kept "the occupier"
　　　　　as the euphemistic
Tour books call him now
　　　　　(for, after all, he's rich)
An easy target
　　　　　in the villages & towns.

Did you swoop right down on him
　　　　　like Marko on the Turks?
You did—
　　　　　but couldn't live with
Certain knowledge
　　　　　of unspeakable reprisals.

Nazi mathematics was
                    a good deal easier
To follow than your theory
                    of recursive functions
Hammered out in hiding
                    six months later in Vienna—
For every officer
                    you blew up in the town
They shot
                    a hundred villagers.
And who is more
                    within his rights
To moralize on firing squads
                    than someone who himself
Would stand before one—
                    Trying you summarily, your
Brothers tied you to a tree
                    and lined up in a nasty file
With leveled rifles aimed
                    to blow your very useful brains
To far less squeamish hills.

You can laugh four decades later
                    since you've lived to tell
The tale:
                    "But my uncle, who as fate
Would have it, is in charge
                    of this grim liquidation,
Couldn't shoot his nephew.
                    That was 1941; two years later
And he would have."
                    He cut you loose and kicked
You in the ass
                    and shouted: *run!*

In the ballad, Vladeta
                    survives to tell the queen
What he saw at Kosovo:
                    "Tell me knight," she says,
"When you were on
                    that wide and level plain
Did you see
                    great Lazar riding by?

91

Did you see my father
                    and my noble brothers there?
Did you see the husbands
                    of my daughters?"
And Vladeta must tell
                    of slaughter and betrayal
—the guslar singing
                    mournfully in lines of just
Ten syllables, sliding over
                    pauses at the fourth
Where prosodists
                    would quickly place
Twin horizontal lines—
                    Yes, Vladeta must tell
The queen exactly what
                    annihilation feels like.

That I see you sometimes
                    standing among memories
Like this other Vladeta
                    before the queen
Or Mestrovich
                    among his early works
Or even like Lord Milosh
                    on that open plain
You find, of course,
                    unspeakably absurd—
"With my broken
                    battle-lance, no doubt,
As all the enemy
                    press in upon me fighting
Near the river Sitnitsa.
                    One account says Milosh
Killed twelve thousand
                    Turkish soldiers after
He had polished off
                    the Sultan. In fact they
Took him in the tent and
                    cut off both his arms!"

You open up the slivovitz
                    and go on with your tales
Which, my friend, for all
                    the jokes and ironies
Required for the telling
                    never cease to bleed—
And in your cups you sing
                    to me Prince Lazar's fatal choice,
You sing the ancient
                    downfall of the Serbs.
"Which Kingdom is it
                    that you long for most?
That's the question that
                    the falcon asked the Tsar.
If you choose the earth, he said
                    then saddle horses,
Tighten girths—
                    have your knights put on
Their swords and make
                    a dawn attack against
The Turks: your enemy
                    will be destroyed.
But if you choose the skies
                    then build a church—
O not of stone
                    but out of silk and velvet—
Gather up your forces,
                    take the bread and wine,
For all shall perish,
                    perish utterly,
And you, O Tsar,
                    shall perish with them."

As you break your words
                    for our inadequate exchange
And give me phrases which
                    in token of their real worth
I give you back in scribbled
                    & devalued English notes
I hear you choose the earth
                    even as you tell me otherwise
And laughingly declare:
                    the skies, the skies!

For you are out there
              on that wide & level plain;
You see yourself
              great Lazar riding by;
You see the father
              of the Lady's brothers there;
You see the husbands
              of her daughters—
And when your uncle
              cuts you loose
You stumble
              through the villages & hills
Playing tokens
              for survival, whispering
In code to border guards
              & agents, prostitutes & poets,
Fellow travelers and
              their wealthy following
Of contraband tobacconists
              an anagram compounded
Of the talismanic words
              that wound the clocks
In old Ragusa:
              OBLITI PRIVATORUM
PUBLICA CURATE—
              Forget your private business
And concern yourself
              with public life, that's
The gist of it—
              knowing well that only those
A man can trust will whisper
              the correct response.
For if a man's a friend
              he knows that underneath
Those proudly chiseled words
              above the lintel close beside
The Rector's palace
              there's a dusty little shop

Whose owner chalks
         (in lingua franca too!)
Upon a blackboard
         hanging in his narrow window
The reply:
         ANYTIME FRIED FISHES.
And that's the phrase,
         you tell me, answers Latin.
That's the phrase
         that took you underground!

Obliti Privatorum Publica Curate
         you intone, and I cry out:
Anytime Fried Fishes!
         and we hug each other like
Two drunken Slavs
         and weep like sentimental
Irishmen & leave our
         empty bottle on the pedestal
Of Mestrovich's well.

Vladeta, my Voyvoda,
         my dear unhappy friend,
There is no Kingdom
         left for us to choose—
Neither of the earth
         nor of the sky.
But peace, peace,
         to all who wander
For whatever reason
         from their stony lands
Bringing all the heavy cargo
         of their legends
Humming in a cipher
         in their lucid, spinning minds!

—John Matthias

Afterword

Poetry fueled the Third Balkan War—specifically, the poetry of the Kosovo Cycle dear to the Serbian people. The passions on display in the fratricidal wars of succession in the former Yugoslavia are embedded in this epic. And it was no accident that a Serbian politician, Slobodan Milošević, discovered in the Kosovo myth the most potent political force of the post–Cold War world—nationalism—a force he used to tear Yugoslavia apart. "The Kosovo heroism does not allow us to forget that at one time we were brave and dignified and one of the few who went into battle undefeated," Milošević announced on 28 June 1989, the six-hundredth anniversary of the Battle of Kosovo. The large crowd assembled on the Field of Blackbirds, where Prince Lazar is said to have traded his earthly crown for the heavenly kingdom, heard these prophetic words from the Serbian strongman: "Six centuries later, again we are in battles and quarrels. They are not armed battles, though such things should not be excluded yet." Another accurate prophecy: during the subsequent fighting in Slovenia, Croatia, and Bosnia-Herzegovina, it was often said that the Yugoslav crisis began in Kosovo, and it would end there.

"What has never been can never be: / One land only but two masters," an anonymous poet argues in *The Battle of Kosovo,* expertly translated by John Matthias and Vladeta Vučković. And for more than a millennium, usually under the yoke of a foreign master, Albanians and Serbs lived side by side, uneasily, in Kosovo, a province the size of Connecticut. Serbs killed thousands of Albanians in the First Balkan War, and Albanians answered the Serbs in kind in World War II. Under Tito, many Serbs emigrated from Kosovo in search of better economic opportunities, and Albanians, with the highest birthrate in Europe, soon outnumbered them by a margin of nine to one—a perilous development for those who regarded Kosovo as their Jerusalem. Schooled in the poetry of Lazar's death and the demise of "a good and ancient Empire," Serbs welcomed Milošević's decision to strip Kosovo of its autonomy in 1990 and purge Albanians from every position of influence.

The Albanians responded by establishing a parallel system of schools, hospitals, and media, seeking to restore their autonomy by nonviolent means, a campaign supplanted in 1998 by the rise of the Kosova Liberation Army (KLA), a guerrilla band agitating for independence. A year of armed conflict between Serbian police and the KLA ensued, in which hundreds of villages were destroyed and hundreds of thousands of Albanians displaced. And the failed peace negotiations at Rambouillet, in France, precipitated NATO's first military action against a sovereign nation. To understand the tenacity of the Serbian people in the face of sustained bombing as well as the ruthlessness with which Serbian forces "ethnically cleansed" Kosovo of its Albanian population one need read no further than these poems, in which "this field of slaughter" was first commemorated—and perhaps prefigured.

Christopher Merrill

96